Practical
Healthy Eating

p^3

This is a P³ Publishing Book
This edition published in 2004

P³ Publishing
Queen Street House
4 Queen Street
Bath BA1 1HE, UK

ISBN: 1-40543-277-2

Printed in China

NOTE

Cup measurements in this book are for American cups.
This book also uses imperial and metric measurements. Follow the same units
of measurement throughout; do not mix imperial and metric.
All spoon measurements are level: teaspoons are assumed to be 5 ml, and
tablespoons are assumed to be 15 ml. Unless otherwise stated,
milk is assumed to be whole milk, eggs and individual vegetables such as potatoes
are medium, and pepper is freshly ground black pepper.

The nutritional information provided for each recipe is per serving or per person.
Optional ingredients, variations, or serving suggestions have not been
included in the calculations. The times given for each recipe are an approximate
guide only because the preparation times may differ according to the techniques used by
different people and the cooking times may vary as a result of the type of oven used.

Recipes using raw or very lightly cooked eggs should be
avoided by infants, the elderly, pregnant women, convalescents,
and anyone suffering from an illness.

Contents

Introduction

Many of us have taken on board the message that what we eat impacts significantly on our health. However, it is easy to become bewildered by the complexities and contradictions in the advice on different foods and dietary regimes that we now face on a daily basis. This book offers a refreshing and inspirational approach to healthy eating based on sound nutritional principles and offers a range of easy-to-prepare yet imaginative recipes. The exciting flavors and textures in these dishes will serve as an antidote to the perceived view that a healthy diet is restrictive. This is food to enjoy as well as to benefit from in terms of promoting good health.

Healthy eating guidelines

In order for your body to maintain itself in good working order, it needs to have a regular and balanced supply of nutrients. This means making the right choice of foods day by day, and nutritionists have developed a way of helping us to make that choice without having to grapple with detailed nutritional data. They have identified the basic food types and divided them into five separate groups. These groups are shown here, with the group we need the most listed first, reducing to those we need least listed last:

Bread, cereals, pasta, noodles, rice, and potatoes

These foods are rich in carbohydrates, which provide the body with energy, and are low in fat. They contain B vitamins, selenium, calcium, and iron as well as fiber. Up to a third of your daily food intake should be chosen from this group.

Vegetables and fruits

These nutritious foods are rich in vitamins, particularly A, C, and E, known as antioxidants, and minerals such as calcium, potassium, magnesium, and iron. They are good sources of fiber and are virtually fat-free. You can eat as many as you like of these, and most health organizations recommend eating at least five portions in total a day.

Meat, poultry, fish, beans, nuts, seeds, and eggs

These foods are our main source of protein, essential for maintaining the body's functions. Meat, poultry, and fish are rich in B vitamins and minerals such as iron, zinc, and magnesium, but they also contain varying amounts of saturated and unsaturated fat.

Milk, cheese, and yogurt

Dairy foods offer good sources of calcium, provide protein, and contain vitamins A, D, and B6 (riboflavin), but they are also high in saturated fats, so consumption needs to be limited. Choosing lower-fat varieties of these foods will help in this way.

Fats and sugars These foods are essential to a healthy diet but they are only needed in small quantities, so they should make up the smallest proportion of your daily food intake. It is preferable to eat more unsaturated fats than saturated fats. Unsaturated fats are found in olive oil and other vegetable oils, oily fish and fish oils, avocados, nuts, and seeds.

Healthy ingredients and options

While the carbohydrate-rich foods are the mainstay of a healthy diet, we need to be wary of falling into the trap of eating them with saturated fats and sugars—for instance, breakfast cereals with sugar and milk, pasta with creamy sauces, bread spread with butter and preserves, or

potatoes in the form of french fries, deep-fried in oil. There are many easy ways to enjoy carbohydrates without counteracting their beneficial effect. For example, opting for whole-wheat or whole-grain varieties of bread, rice, pasta, and breakfast cereals will maximize your intake of dietary fiber and vitamins.

Variety is the key to getting the most from vegetables and fruits in your diet, in terms both of the different nutrients they have and their fiber content, in addition to taste and texture. Bananas, for instance, are rich in potassium, which can help to regulate blood pressure, and citrus fruits are high in fiber and vitamin C. Spinach, carrots, and bell peppers offer beta-carotene, which the body converts into vitamin A. Some studies have found that lycopene, which gives tomatoes their bright red coloring, can help to reduce the risk of prostate cancer in men, and possibly cervical cancer in women. It appears that canned or otherwise processed tomatoes are even more beneficial than the fresh variety.

You can avoid loss of vitamins from vegetables and fruits by taking a few simple steps in their preparation. Avoid peeling them where possible, avoid letting them stand in water before cooking, and avoid overcooking them. Where possible, steam or bake them, or simmer in a minimal amount of water.

Your choice of protein source has an important part to play in maintaining a healthy diet. Skinless turkey and chicken are relatively low in fat, particularly saturated fats, although the brown meat is fattier than the white. Lean cuts of pork are surprisingly low in fat—more so than beef or lamb. While white fish is low in fat, oily fish such as salmon, tuna, mackerel, herrings, sardines, and anchovies contains omega-3 fatty acids, which are thought to be protective against heart disease and strokes, and may be helpful for those suffering from psoriasis or arthritis. Canned varieties are no less beneficial in this respect. Bean curd is a particularly healthy protein source: it is low in saturated fat and cholesterol and contains protective antioxidants. Dried beans, peas, and lentils are another good, lowfat source of protein, but they are best

served with whole-grain and plant foods to provide the correct balance of nutrients, particularly within a vegetarian diet. Nuts are high in fat, but it is mostly of the unsaturated kind, which, rather than raising blood cholesterol levels, may even help to reduce them. Hazelnuts, walnuts, and almonds are good choices.

Fatty foods are seductive because the fats and oils they contain are phenomenal flavor-boosters. However, other healthier ingredients can be used in place of fats to contribute to the taste of dishes, such as fresh herbs, including garlic and fresh gingerroot, dried herbs, spices, tomato paste, olives, capers, reduced-salt soy sauce, Worcestershire sauce, Tabasco sauce, bouillon, vegetable and fruit juices, and wine.

Healthy cooking methods

Once you have chosen the right foods for a healthy, balanced diet, it is vital to follow through with a healthy approach to cooking them. Steaming requires no additional fat and retains nutrients and flavor, while broiling, grilling, or griddling (using a dry cast-iron or aluminum griddle pan on the stovetop) also seals in flavor with little or no need for fat.

Rapidly stir-frying foods in a wok in a minimal amount of oil is also a relatively healthy cooking method, and again maximizes the taste and texture of ingredients. Microwaving is also a fat-free cooking method. Using a heavy-bottomed, nonstick skillet, you can dry-fry ground meat or bacon, thereby

releasing its own fat, which can then be drained away. Use a proprietary oil spray for pan-frying, or alternatively, try "sautéeing" vegetables without any additional fat in a covered pan, where they will cook in their own juices.

KEY	
🍴	Simplicity level 1–3 (1 easiest, 3 slightly harder)
🍲	Preparation time
🕐	Cooking time

Bacon, Bean & Garlic Soup

This is a mouthwatering and healthy vegetable, bean, and bacon soup, which you can cook in a microwave oven. Serve it with whole-wheat bread.

NUTRITIONAL INFORMATION

Calories	261	Sugars	. . . . .5g
Protein	. . . . .23g	Fat	. . . . .8g
Carbohydrate	. . .25g	Saturates	. . . . . .2g

5 mins   20 mins

SERVES 4

I N G R E D I E N T S

8 oz/225 g lean smoked back bacon slices

1 carrot, thinly sliced

1 celery stalk, thinly sliced

1 onion, chopped

1 tbsp oil

3 garlic cloves, sliced

3 cups hot vegetable bouillon

7 oz/200 g canned chopped tomatoes

1 tbsp chopped fresh thyme

about 14 oz/400 g canned cannellini beans, drained

1 tbsp tomato paste

salt and pepper

grated colby cheese, to garnish

COOK'S TIP

For a more substantial soup, add 2¼ oz/60 g small pasta shapes or short lengths of spaghetti when you add the bouillon and tomatoes. You will also need to add an extra ⅔ cup vegetable bouillon.

1 Chop 2 slices of the bacon and place in a microwave-proof bowl. Microwave on High power for 3–4 minutes, until the fat runs out and the bacon is well cooked. Stir the bacon halfway through cooking to separate the pieces. Transfer to a plate lined with paper towels and let cool. When cool, the bacon pieces should be crisp and dry. Place the carrot, celery, onion, and oil in a microwave-proof bowl. Cover and cook on High power for 4 minutes.

2 Chop the remaining bacon and add to the bowl with the garlic. Cover and cook on High power for 2 minutes.

3 Add the bouillon, the contents of the can of tomatoes, the thyme, beans, and tomato paste. Cover and cook on High power for 8 minutes, stirring halfway through. Season to taste. Ladle the soup into warmed bowls and sprinkle with the crisp bacon and grated cheese.

Red Lentil Soup with Yogurt

This tasty red lentil soup flavored with chopped cilantro is an easy microwave dish. The yogurt adds a light piquancy to the soup.

NUTRITIONAL INFORMATION

Calories 280   Sugars 6g
Protein . . . . .17g   Fat 7g
Carbohydrate . . .40g   Saturates 4g

5 mins   30 mins

SERVES 4

I N G R E D I E N T S

2 tbsp butter

1 onion, finely chopped

1 celery stalk, finely chopped

1 large carrot, grated

1 bay leaf

1 cup red lentils

5 cups hot vegetable bouillon or
   chicken bouillon

2 tbsp chopped fresh cilantro

4 tbsp lowfat plain yogurt

salt and pepper

sprigs of fresh cilantro, to garnish

1   Place the butter, onion, and celery in a microwave-proof bowl. Cover and microwave on High power for 3 minutes.

2   Add the carrot, bay leaf, and lentils. Pour in the bouillon. Cover and cook on High power for 15 minutes, stirring halfway through.

3   Remove the bowl from the microwave oven, cover, and stand for 5 minutes.

4   Remove and discard the bay leaf, then process, in batches, in a food processor, until smooth. Alternatively, press the soup through a strainer.

5   Pour the soup into a clean bowl. Season with salt and pepper to taste and stir in the cilantro. Cover and microwave on High power for 4–5 minutes, until the soup is piping hot.

6   Serve in warmed soup bowls. Stir 1 tablespoon of yogurt into each serving and garnish with small sprigs of fresh cilantro.

COOK'S TIP

For an extra creamy soup, try using lowfat crème fraîche or sour cream instead of yogurt.

Crudités with Shrimp Sauce

In this delicious yet lowfat recipe, fruit and vegetable crudités are served with a spicy, garlicky shrimp sauce.

NUTRITIONAL INFORMATION			
Calories	.85	Sugars	11g
Protein	7g	Fat	1g
Carbohydrate	12g	Saturates	0.2g

12¼ hrs   0 mins

SERVES 4

INGREDIENTS

about 1 lb 10 oz/750 g prepared
raw fruit and vegetables, such
as broccoli, cauliflower, apple,
pineapple, cucumber, celery, bell
peppers, and mushrooms

SAUCE

2¼ oz/60 g dried shrimp

½-inch/1-cm cube shrimp paste

3 garlic cloves, crushed

4 red chiles, seeded and chopped

6 stems fresh cilantro, coarsely chopped

juice of 2 limes

fish sauce, to taste

brown sugar, to taste

1 To make the sauce, put the dried shrimp in a bowl of warm water and soak for 10 minutes.

2 Place the shrimp paste, drained shrimp, garlic, chiles, and cilantro in a food processor or blender and process until well chopped but not smooth.

3 Turn the sauce mixture into a bowl and add the lime juice, mixing well.

4 Add fish sauce and brown sugar to taste, then mix well.

5 Cover the bowl tightly and chill the sauce in the refrigerator for at least 12 hours, or overnight.

6 To serve, arrange the fruit and vegetables attractively on a large serving plate. Place the prepared sauce in the center for dipping.

COOK'S TIP

Hard-cooked quail's eggs can be added to this traditional fruit and vegetable platter to create a dish for a special occasion.

Vegetables with Sesame Dip

This tasty dip is great for livening up simply cooked vegetables. Varying the vegetables according to the season adds interest to the dish.

NUTRITIONAL INFORMATION

Calories 126	Sugars 7g	
Protein 11g	Fat 6g	
Carbohydrate 8g	Saturates 1g	

5 mins   20 mins

SERVES 4

INGREDIENTS

2½ cups small broccoli florets

2 cups small cauliflower florets

8 oz/225 g asparagus, sliced into 2-inch/
5-cm lengths

2 small red onions, cut into fourths

1 tbsp lime juice

2 tsp toasted sesame seeds

1 tbsp chopped fresh chives, to garnish

HOT SESAME & GARLIC DIP

1 tsp sunflower oil

2 garlic cloves, crushed

½–1 tsp chili powder

2 tsp sesame seed paste (tahini)

⅔ cup lowfat unsweetened yogurt

2 tbsp chopped fresh chives

salt and pepper

1 Line the bottom of a steamer with baking parchment and arrange the broccoli florets, cauliflower florets, asparagus, and onion pieces on top.

2 Bring a wok or large pan of water to a boil, and place the steamer on top. Sprinkle the vegetables with lime juice and steam them for 10 minutes, or until they are just tender.

3 To make the Hot Sesame & Garlic Dip, heat the oil in a small, nonstick pan, add the garlic, chili powder, and seasoning to taste, and cook gently for 2–3 minutes, until the garlic is soft.

4 Remove the pan from the heat and stir in the sesame seed paste and yogurt. Return the pan to the heat and cook gently for 1–2 minutes without bringing to a boil. Stir in the chives.

5 Remove the vegetables from the steamer and place on a warmed serving platter. Sprinkle them with the sesame seeds and garnish with chopped chives. Serve with the hot dip.

Mixed Bean & Apple Salad

Use any mixture of beans you have at hand in this recipe, but the wider the variety, the more colorful the salad.

NUTRITIONAL INFORMATION	
Calories 183	Sugars 8g
Protein 6g	Fat 7g
Carbohydrate ...26g	Saturates 1g

20 mins   20 mins

SERVES 4

INGREDIENTS

8 oz/225 g new potatoes, scrubbed and cut into fourths

8 oz/225 g mixed canned beans, such as red kidney beans, small cannellini beans, and borlotti beans, drained and rinsed

1 red eating apple, diced and tossed in 1 tbsp lemon juice

1 yellow bell pepper, seeded and diced

1 shallot, sliced

½ fennel bulb, sliced

oakleaf lettuce leaves

DRESSING

1 tbsp red wine vinegar

2 tbsp olive oil

1½ tsp mild yellow mustard

1 garlic clove, crushed

2 tsp chopped fresh thyme

1 Cook the potatoes in a pan of boiling water for 15 minutes, until tender. Drain and transfer to a large bowl.

2 Add the mixed beans to the potatoes, with the diced apple, yellow bell pepper, and sliced shallot and fennel. Mix thoroughly, taking care not to break up the cooked potatoes.

3 To make the dressing, whisk all the dressing ingredients together until thoroughly combined, then pour it over the potato salad.

4 Line a serving plate or salad bowl with the oakleaf lettuce leaves and spoon the potato mixture into the center. Serve the salad immediately.

VARIATION

Use Dijon or whole-grain mustard in place of mild yellow mustard for a different flavor.

Broccoli & Almond Salad

This is a colorful, crunchy salad with a delicious dressing. It is better left overnight if possible for the flavors to mingle.

NUTRITIONAL INFORMATION

Calories 181	Sugars 7g
Protein 9g	Fat 12g
Carbohydrate 9g	Saturates 2g

4½ hrs   10 mins

SERVES 4

INGREDIENTS

1 lb/450 g small broccoli florets

1¾ oz/50 g baby corn cobs, halved lengthwise

1 red bell pepper, seeded and cut into thin strips

1¾ oz/50 g blanched almonds

DRESSING

1 tbsp sesame seeds

1 tbsp peanut oil

2 garlic cloves, crushed

2 tbsp light soy sauce

1 tbsp clear honey

2 tsp lemon juice

pepper

lemon zest, to garnish (optional)

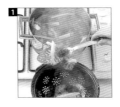

1 Blanch the broccoli and baby corn cobs in boiling water for 5 minutes. Drain well, rinse, and drain again.

2 Transfer the broccoli and baby corn cobs to a large mixing bowl and add the bell pepper and almonds.

3 To make the dressing, heat a wok and add the sesame seeds. Dry-fry, stirring constantly, for about 1 minute, or until the sesame seeds are lightly browned and are giving off a delicious aroma.

4 Mix the peanut oil, garlic, soy sauce, honey, lemon juice, and pepper in a bowl. Add the sesame seeds and mix well.

5 Pour the dressing over the salad, cover with plastic wrap, and set aside in the refrigerator for a minimum of 4 hours and preferably overnight.

6 Garnish the salad with lemon zest (if using) and serve.

COOK'S TIP

Take care when browning the sesame seeds, because they will quickly burn. Dry-fry over low heat and stir constantly.

Rice with Fruit & Nuts

Here is a tasty and filling rice dish that is nice and spicy and includes fruits for a refreshing flavor and toasted nuts for a crunchy texture.

NUTRITIONAL INFORMATION

Calories 423	Sugars 19g	
Protein 10g	Fat 17g	
Carbohydrate . . .62g	Saturates 2g	

20 mins   1 hr

SERVES 6

INGREDIENTS

4 tbsp vegetable ghee or vegetable oil

1 large onion, chopped

2 garlic cloves, crushed

1-inch/2.5-cm piece of fresh gingerroot, chopped

1 tsp chili powder

1 tsp cumin seeds

1 tbsp mild or medium curry powder or paste

1½ cups brown rice

3½ cups boiling vegetable bouillon

14 oz/400 g canned chopped tomatoes

1½ cups ready-to-eat dried apricots or peaches, cut into slivers

1 red bell pepper, seeded and diced

¾ cup frozen peas

1–2 small, slightly green bananas

½–¾ cup toasted nuts, such as almonds, cashews, and hazelnuts or pine nuts

salt and pepper

sprigs of fresh cilantro, to garnish

1 Heat the ghee or oil in a large pan. Add the onion and cook over low heat for 3 minutes. Stir in the garlic, ginger, spices, and rice and cook gently, stirring constantly, for 2 minutes, until the rice is coated in the spiced oil.

2 Pour in the boiling bouillon, add the chopped tomatoes, and season with salt and pepper to taste. Bring to a boil, then lower the heat, cover, and simmer gently for 40 minutes, or until the rice is almost cooked and most of the liquid has been absorbed.

3 Add the slivered apricots or peaches, diced red bell pepper, and peas. Cover and continue cooking for 10 minutes. Remove from the heat and set aside for 5 minutes without uncovering.

4 Peel and slice the bananas. Uncover the rice mixture and fork through to mix the ingredients and fluff up the rice. Add the sliced bananas and toasted nuts and toss lightly. Transfer to a warmed serving platter and garnish with sprigs of fresh cilantro. Serve immediately.

Spinach & Nut Pilau

Fragrant basmati rice is cooked with porcini mushrooms, spinach, and pistachios in this easy microwave recipe.

55 mins   15–20 mins

SERVES 4

I N G R E D I E N T S

¼ oz/10 g dried porcini mushrooms

1¼ cups hot water

1 onion, chopped

1 garlic clove, crushed

1 tsp grated gingerroot

½ fresh green chile, seeded and chopped

2 tbsp oil

1¼ cups basmati rice

1 large carrot, grated

¾ cup vegetable bouillon

½ tsp ground cinnamon

4 cloves

½ tsp saffron strands

8 oz/225 g fresh spinach, long
   stalks removed

½ cup pistachios

1 tbsp chopped fresh cilantro

salt and pepper

fresh cilantro leaves, to garnish

1 Place the porcini mushrooms in a small bowl. Pour over the hot water and let soak for 30 minutes.

2 Place the onion, garlic, ginger, chile, and oil in a microwave-proof bowl. Cover and microwave on High power for 2 minutes. Rinse the rice, then stir it into the bowl, together with the carrot. Cover and cook on High power for 1 minute.

3 Strain and coarsely chop the mushrooms. Add enough mushroom soaking liquid to the bouillon to make 1¾ cups. Pour onto the rice.

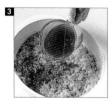

4 Stir in the mushrooms, cinnamon, cloves, saffron, and ½ teaspoon salt. Cover and cook on High power for 10 minutes, stirring once. Let the mixture stand, covered, for 10 minutes.

5 Place the spinach in another microwave-proof bowl. Cover and cook on High power for 3½ minutes, stirring once. Drain well and chop the spinach coarsely.

6 Stir the spinach, pistachios, and chopped cilantro into the rice. Season to taste with salt and pepper and garnish with cilantro leaves. Serve immediately.

Gorgonzola & Pumpkin Pizza

Blue Gorgonzola cheese and juicy pears combine to give a colorful pizza. The whole-wheat base adds a nutty flavor and texture.

NUTRITIONAL INFORMATION	
Calories 470	Sugars 5g
Protein 17g	Fat 15g
Carbohydrate . . .72g	Saturates 6g

🍲 1¼ hrs   🕐 35 mins

SERVES 4

I N G R E D I E N T S

PIZZA DOUGH

2 tsp dry yeast

1 tsp sugar

1 cup lukewarm water

1¼ cups whole-wheat all-purpose flour

1¼ cups white bread flour

1 tsp salt

1 tbsp olive oil, plus extra for greasing

TOPPING

1 lb/450 g pumpkin or squash, peeled and cubed

1 tbsp olive oil

1 pear, cored, peeled, and sliced

1 cup crumbled Gorgonzola cheese

fresh rosemary, to garnish

1 To make the dough, place the yeast and sugar in a pitcher and mix with 4 tablespoons of the lukewarm water. Let the yeast mixture stand in a warm place for 15 minutes, or until foamy.

2 Combine both of the flours with the salt and make a well in the center. Add the oil, the yeast mixture, and the remaining water. Using a wooden spoon, mix to form a dough.

3 Turn the dough out onto a floured counter and knead for 4–5 minutes, or until smooth.

4 Return the dough to the bowl, cover with an oiled sheet of plastic wrap, and let rise for 30 minutes, or until doubled in size.

5 Remove the dough from the bowl. Knead the dough for 2 minutes. Using a rolling pin, roll out the dough to form a long oval shape, then place it on an oiled cookie sheet, pushing out the edges until even. The dough should be no more than ¼ inch/5 mm thick because it will rise during cooking.

6 To make the topping, place the pumpkin in a shallow roasting pan. Drizzle with the olive oil and cook under a preheated broiler for 20 minutes, or until soft and lightly golden.

7 Top the dough with the pumpkin and pear, brushing with the oil from the pan. Scatter over the Gorgonzola. Bake in a preheated oven, 400°F/200°C, for about 15 minutes, or until the base is golden. Garnish with fresh rosemary.

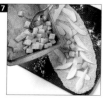

Bean Curd with Mushrooms

Chinese mushrooms are available from Chinese food stores
and health food stores and add a unique flavor to Asian dishes.

NUTRITIONAL INFORMATION

Calories 218	Sugars 1g	
Protein 12g	Fat 14g	
Carbohydrate . . .13g	Saturates 2g	

15 mins   15 mins

SERVES 4

INGREDIENTS

1 oz/25 g dried Chinese mushrooms

1 lb/450 g firm bean curd

4 tbsp cornstarch

oil, for deep-frying

2 garlic cloves, finely chopped

2 tsp grated fresh gingerroot

1 cup frozen or fresh peas

1 Place the Chinese mushrooms in a large heatproof bowl. Pour in enough boiling water to cover and let stand for about 10 minutes.

2 Meanwhile, using a sharp knife, cut the bean curd into bite-size cubes.

3 Place the cornstarch in a large bowl. Add the bean curd to the bowl and toss in the cornstarch until evenly coated.

4 Heat the oil for deep-frying in a large preheated wok.

5 Add the cubes of bean curd to the wok and then deep-fry them, in batches, for about 2–3 minutes, or until they are golden and crispy. Remove the bean curd with a slotted spoon and drain on paper towels.

6 Drain off all but 2 tablespoons of oil from the wok. Add the garlic, ginger, and Chinese mushrooms to the wok and cook for 2–3 minutes.

7 Return the cooked bean curd to the wok and add the peas. Heat through for 1 minute then serve hot.

COOK'S TIP
Chinese dried mushrooms add flavor and a distinctive aroma. They are sold dried in packages, and they can be expensive, but only a few are needed per dish and they store indefinitely. If they are unavailable, use open-cap mushrooms instead.

Yucatan Fish

Herbs, onion, green bell pepper, and pumpkin seeds are used to flavor this baked fish, which is first marinated in lime juice.

NUTRITIONAL INFORMATION

Calories	248	Sugars	.........2g
Protein	........33g	Fat	...........11g
Carbohydrate	....3g	Saturates	......1g

40 mins   35 mins

SERVES 4

I N G R E D I E N T S

4 cod cutlets or steaks, or hake cutlets (about 6 oz/175 g each)

2 tbsp lime juice

1 green bell pepper

1 tbsp olive oil

1 onion, finely chopped

1–2 garlic cloves, crushed

1½ oz/40 g green pumpkin seeds

grated rind of ½ lime

1 tbsp chopped fresh cilantro or parsley

1 tbsp chopped fresh mixed herbs

2¼ oz/60 g button mushrooms, thinly sliced

2–3 tbsp fresh orange juice or white wine

salt and pepper

T O   G A R N I S H

lime wedges

fresh mixed herbs

1 Wipe the fish, place in a shallow, ovenproof dish, and pour over the lime juice. Turn the fish in the juice, season with salt and pepper, cover, and let stand in a cool place for 15–30 minutes.

2 Halve the bell pepper, remove the seeds, and place under a preheated moderate broiler, skin-side upward, until the skin burns and splits. Let cool slightly, then peel off the skin and chop the flesh.

3 Heat the oil in a pan and cook the onion, garlic, bell pepper, and pumpkin seeds gently for a few minutes, until the onion is soft.

4 Stir in the lime rind, cilantro or parsley, mixed herbs, mushrooms, and seasoning, and spoon over the fish.

5 Spoon or pour the orange juice or wine over the fish, cover with foil or a lid, and place in a preheated oven, 350°F/180°C, for about 30 minutes, or until the fish is just tender.

6 Remove the fish from the oven, garnish with lime wedges and fresh mixed herbs, and serve.

Fish & Yogurt Quenelles

These quenelles, made from a thick puree of fish and yogurt, can be prepared well in advance and stored in the refrigerator before poaching.

NUTRITIONAL INFORMATION

Calories	228	Sugars	.........7g
Protein	........39g	Fat	..........2g
Carbohydrate	...14g	Saturates	......1g

45 mins   15 mins

SERVES 4

INGREDIENTS

1 lb 10 oz/750 g white fish fillets, such as cod, coley, or whiting, skinned

2 small egg whites

½ tsp ground coriander

1 tsp ground mace

⅔ cup lowfat plain yogurt

1 small onion, sliced

salt and pepper

mixture of boiled basmati rice and wild rice, to serve

SAUCE

1 bunch of watercress (or baby spinach if watercress is unavailable), trimmed

1¼ cups chicken bouillon

2 tbsp cornstarch

⅔ cup lowfat plain yogurt

2 tbsp lowfat crème fraîche (or plain yogurt, if crème fraîche is unavailable)

1 Cut the fish into pieces and process it in a food processor for 30 seconds. Add the egg whites and process for another 30 seconds to a stiff paste. Add the coriander, mace, yogurt, and seasoning, and process until smooth. Cover and chill for at least 30 minutes.

2 Spoon the mixture into a pastry bag, and pipe into sausage shapes about 4 inches/10 cm long. Alternatively, take rounded dessertspoons of the mixture and shape into ovals using 2 spoons.

3 Bring about 2 inches/5 cm of water to a boil in a skillet and add the onion. Lower the quenelles into the water, using a spatula or spoon. Cover the pan and poach for 8 minutes, turning once. Remove with a slotted spoon and drain.

4 Chop the watercress or baby spinach, reserving a few sprigs for the garnish. Process the remainder with the bouillon, then pour into a small pan. Stir the cornstarch into the yogurt, and then pour into the pan. Bring to a boil, stirring. Stir in the crème fraîche or yogurt, season, and remove from the heat. Garnish with the watercress or baby spinach, and serve with cooked basmati and wild rice.

Balti Cod & Red Lentils

The anise in this recipe gives a very delicate aroma to the fish and really enhances the flavor. Serve with whole-wheat bread.

NUTRITIONAL INFORMATION

Calories	236	Sugars	.........3g
Protein	........29g	Fat	...........7g
Carbohydrate	...15g	Saturates	......1g

5 mins   1 hr

SERVES 4

INGREDIENTS

2 tbsp oil

¼ tsp ground asafetida (optional)

1 tbsp crushed anise

1 tsp ground ginger

1 tsp chili powder

¼ tsp ground turmeric

1 cup split red lentils

1 tsp salt

1 lb 2 oz/500 g cod, skinned, filleted, and cut into 1-inch/2.5-cm cubes

1 fresh red chile, chopped

3 tbsp lowfat plain yogurt

2 tbsp chopped fresh cilantro

whole-wheat bread, to serve

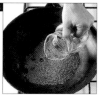

1 Heat the oil in a Balti pan or wok, add the asafetida (if using), and cook for about 10 seconds to burn off the smell of the asafetida.

2 Add the anise, ginger, chili powder, and turmeric and cook for 30 seconds.

3 Wash the lentils thoroughly, then add to the pan with the salt and enough water to cover.

4 Bring to a boil, then simmer gently for 45 minutes, until the lentils are soft but not mushy.

5 Add the cod pieces and chopped red chile, bring to a boil, and simmer for another 10 minutes.

6 Stir in the yogurt and fresh cilantro into the fish mixture and serve with warm whole-wheat bread.

COOK'S TIP

Ground asafetida is easier to use than the type that comes in a block. It should only be used in small quantities. Do not be put off by the smell, which is very pungent.

Salmon Fillet with Herbs

This is a great party dish. The salmon is cooked with fennel, and the combination of the herbs and barbecue flavor make it truly irresistible.

NUTRITIONAL INFORMATION

Calories	507	Sugars	. . . . . . .0.4g
Protein	. . . . .46g	Fat	. . . . .35g
Carbohydrate	. . .0.5g	Saturates	. . . . . .6g

5 mins   30 mins

SERVES 4

INGREDIENTS

½ large bunch dried thyme

5 fresh rosemary branches, 6–8 inches/
15–20 cm long

8 bay leaves

2 lb 4 oz/1 kg salmon fillet

1 bulb fennel, cut into 8 pieces

2 tbsp lemon juice

2 tbsp olive oil

TO SERVE

crusty bread

fresh salad greens

1 Make a base on a hot barbecue grill with the dried thyme, rosemary branches, and bay leaves, overlapping them so that they cover a slightly larger area than the salmon.

2 Carefully place the salmon on top of the herbs.

3 Arrange the fennel around the edge of the fish.

4 Combine the lemon juice and oil and brush the salmon with it.

5 Cover the salmon loosely with a piece of foil, to keep it moist.

6 Cook for about 20–30 minutes, basting frequently with the lemon juice mixture.

7 Remove the salmon from the barbecue grill, cut it into slices, and serve with the fennel.

8 Serve with slices of crusty bread and fresh salad greens.

VARIATION

Use whatever combination of herbs you may have at hand—but avoid the stronger tasting herbs, such as sage and marjoram, which are unsuitable for fish.

Chicken Tikka Kabobs

Chicken tikka is a lowfat Indian dish. Recipes vary, but you can try your own combination of spices to suit your personal taste.

NUTRITIONAL INFORMATION	
Calories 191	Sugars 8g
Protein 30g	Fat 4g
Carbohydrate 8g	Saturates 2g

🍲 2¼ hrs   🕐 15 mins

SERVES 4

INGREDIENTS

4 skinless, boneless chicken breast portions, about 4½ oz/125 g each

1 garlic clove, crushed

1 tsp grated fresh gingerroot

1 fresh green chile, seeded and finely chopped

6 tbsp lowfat plain yogurt

1 tbsp tomato paste

1 tsp ground cumin

1 tsp ground coriander

1 tsp ground turmeric

1 large ripe mango

1 tbsp lime juice

salt and pepper

fresh cilantro leaves, to garnish

TO SERVE

boiled white rice

lime wedges

mixed salad greens

warmed nan bread

1 Cut the chicken into 1-inch/2.5-cm cubes and place in a shallow dish.

2 Combine the garlic, ginger, chile, yogurt, tomato paste, spices, and seasoning. Spoon over the chicken, cover, and chill for 2 hours.

3 Using a vegetable peeler, peel the skin from the mango. Slice down either side of the pit and cut the mango flesh into cubes. Toss in lime juice, cover, and chill until required.

4 Thread the chicken and mango pieces alternately onto 8 skewers. Place the skewers on a broiler rack and brush the chicken with the yogurt marinade and the lime juice left from the mango.

5 Place under a preheated moderate broiler and cook for 6–7 minutes. Turn over, brush again with the marinade and lime juice, and cook for 6–7 minutes, until the juices run clear when the chicken is pierced with a sharp knife.

6 Serve the kabobs immediately on a bed of rice on a warmed platter, garnished with fresh cilantro leaves and accompanied by lime wedges, mixed salad greens, and warmed nan bread.

Steamed Chicken Parcels

A healthy recipe with a delicate Asian flavor. Use large spinach leaves to wrap around the chicken, but make sure they are young leaves.

NUTRITIONAL INFORMATION

Calories 216	Sugars 7g
Protein 31g	Fat 7g
Carbohydrate 7g	Saturates 2g

20 mins 30 mins

SERVES 4

INGREDIENTS

4 lean, skinless, boneless chicken breasts

1 tsp ground lemongrass

2 scallions, finely chopped

9 oz/250 g young carrots

9 oz/250 g young zucchini

2 stalks celery

1 tsp light soy sauce

9 oz/250 g spinach leaves

2 tsp sesame oil

salt and pepper

1 With a sharp knife, make a slit through one side of each chicken breast, to open out a large pocket.

2 Sprinkle the inside of the pocket with lemongrass, and salt and pepper. Tuck the scallions into the chicken pockets.

3 Trim the carrots, zucchini, and celery, then cut into small matchsticks. Plunge them into a pan of boiling water for 1 minute, then drain and toss in the soy sauce.

4 Pack the mixture into the pockets in the chicken breasts and fold over firmly to enclose it. Reserve the remaining vegetables. Wash and dry the spinach leaves, then wrap the chicken breasts firmly in the leaves to enclose completely. If the leaves are too firm, steam them for a few seconds, until softened and flexible.

5 Place the wrapped chicken in a steamer and then steam over rapidly boiling water for about 20–25 minutes, depending on size.

6 Stir-fry any leftover vegetable sticks and spinach for 1–2 minutes in the sesame oil and serve with the chicken.

Mustard Baked Chicken

In this dish, chicken pieces are cooked in a succulent mild mustard sauce, coated in poppy seeds, and served on a bed of fresh pasta shells.

NUTRITIONAL INFORMATION	
Calories 652	Sugars 5g
Protein 51g	Fat 31g
Carbohydrate . . .46g	Saturates 12g

10 mins   35 mins

SERVES 4

I N G R E D I E N T S

8 chicken pieces, 4 oz/115 g each

4 tbsp butter, melted

4 tbsp mild mustard (see Cook's Tip)

2 tbsp lemon juice

1 tbsp brown sugar

1 tsp paprika

3 tbsp poppy seeds

14 oz/400 g dried pasta shells

1 tbsp olive oil

salt and pepper

1 Arrange the chicken pieces in a single layer in a large ovenproof dish.

2 Combine the butter, mustard, lemon juice, brown sugar, and paprika in a bowl and season with salt and pepper to taste. Brush the mixture over the upper

surfaces of the chicken pieces and then bake in a preheated oven, 400°F/200°C, for 15 minutes.

3 Remove the dish from the oven and carefully turn over the chicken pieces. Coat the upper surfaces of the chicken with the remaining mustard mixture, sprinkle the chicken pieces with poppy seeds, and return to the oven for another 15 minutes.

4 Meanwhile, bring a large pan of lightly salted water to a boil. Add the pasta shells and olive oil, bring back to a boil, and cook for 8–10 minutes, or until tender but still firm to the bite.

5 Drain the pasta thoroughly and arrange on a warm serving dish. Top the pasta with the chicken pieces, pour the mustard sauce over them, and serve immediately.

COOK'S TIP

Dijon is the type of mustard most often used in cooking, because it has a clean and mildly spicy flavor. German mustard has a sweet-sour taste, and Bavarian mustard is slightly sweeter. American mustard is mild and sweet.

Orange Turkey with Rice

This is a good way to use up leftover rice. Use fresh or canned sweet pink grapefruit for an interesting alternative to the orange.

NUTRITIONAL INFORMATION

Calories 337	Sugars 12g
Protein 32g	Fat 7g
Carbohydrate 40g	Saturates 1g

30 mins   40 mins

SERVES 4

I N G R E D I E N T S

1 tbsp olive oil

1 medium onion, chopped

1 lb/450 g skinless lean turkey (such as fillet), cut into thin strips

1¼ cups unsweetened orange juice

1 bay leaf

8 oz/225 g small broccoli florets

1 large zucchini, diced

1 large orange

6 cups cooked brown rice

salt and pepper

tomato and onion salad, to serve

TO GARNISH

1 oz/25 g pitted black olives in brine, drained and cut into fourths

shredded basil leaves

1 Heat the oil in a large skillet and cook the onion and turkey, stirring, for 4–5 minutes, until lightly browned.

2 Pour in the orange juice and add the bay leaf and seasoning. Bring to a boil and simmer for 10 minutes.

3 Meanwhile, bring a large pan of water to a boil and cook the broccoli florets, covered, for 2 minutes. Add the diced zucchini, then bring back to a boil. Cover and cook for another 3 minutes. Do not overcook. Drain and set aside.

4 Using a sharp knife, peel off the skin and white pith from the orange. Slice down the orange to make thin circular slices, then halve each slice.

5 Stir the broccoli, zucchini, rice, and orange slices into the turkey mixture.

Gently mix together and season, then heat through for another 3–4 minutes, or until the mixture is piping hot.

6 Transfer the turkey rice to warm serving plates and garnish with black olives and shredded basil leaves. Serve the turkey with a fresh tomato and onion salad.

Fruity Duck Stir-Fry

The pineapple and plum sauce add a sweetness and fruity flavor to this colorful recipe, which blends well with the duck.

NUTRITIONAL INFORMATION	
Calories 241	Sugars 7g
Protein 26g	Fat 8g
Carbohydrate . . .16g	Saturates 2g

🍲 5 mins   🕐 25 mins

SERVES 4

INGREDIENTS

4 duck breasts

1 tsp Chinese five-spice powder

1 tbsp cornstarch

1 tbsp chili oil

8 oz/225 g pearl onions, peeled

2 garlic cloves, crushed

3½ oz/100 g baby corn cobs

1¼ cups canned pineapple chunks

6 scallions, sliced

1 cup bean sprouts

2 tbsp plum sauce

1 Remove any skin from the duck breasts. Cut the duck into thin slices.

2 Mix the Chinese five-spice powder and the cornstarch. Toss the duck in the mixture, until well coated.

3 Heat the oil in a preheated wok. Cook the duck for 10 minutes, or until just beginning to go crisp around the edges. Remove from the wok and set aside.

4 Add the onions and garlic to the wok and cook for 5 minutes, or until softened. Add the baby corn cobs and cook for another 5 minutes. Add the pineapple, scallions, and bean sprouts and cook for 3–4 minutes. Stir in the plum sauce.

5 Return the cooked duck to the wok and toss until well mixed. Transfer to warm serving dishes and serve hot.

COOK'S TIP

Buy pineapple chunks in natural juice rather than syrup for a fresher flavor. If you can only obtain pineapple in syrup, rinse it in cold water, and drain thoroughly before using.

Stir-Fried Beef & Beans

In this recipe the green of the beans complements the dark color of the beef, and everything is served in a rich sauce.

NUTRITIONAL INFORMATION

Calories 381	Sugars 3g
Protein 25g	Fat 27g
Carbohydrate . . .10g	Saturates 8g

🥚 35 mins   🕐 15 mins

SERVES 4

I N G R E D I E N T S

1 lb/450 g beef fillet steak or rump steak,
cut into 1-inch/2.5-cm pieces

M A R I N A D E

2 tsp cornstarch

2 tbsp dark soy sauce

2 tsp peanut oil

S A U C E

2 tbsp vegetable oil

3 garlic cloves, crushed

1 small onion, cut into 8 pieces

8 oz/225 g thin green beans, halved

¼ cup unsalted cashews

1 oz/25 g canned bamboo shoots, drained

2 tsp dark soy sauce

2 tsp Chinese rice wine or dry sherry

½ cup beef bouillon

2 tsp cornstarch

4 tsp water

salt and pepper

 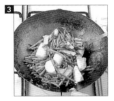 

1 To make the marinade, mix together thoroughly the cornstarch, soy sauce, and peanut oil.

2 Place the steak in a shallow glass bowl. Pour the marinade over the steak, turn to coat thoroughly, cover, and marinate in the refrigerator for at least 30 minutes—the longer the better.

3 To make the sauce, heat the oil in a preheated wok. Add the garlic, onion, green beans, cashews, and bamboo shoots, and cook for 2–3 minutes.

4 Remove the steak from the marinade, drain, add to the wok, and cook for 3–4 minutes.

5 Mix together the soy sauce, Chinese rice wine or sherry, and beef bouillon. Blend the cornstarch with the water and stir into the soy sauce mixture, mixing everything well to combine.

6 Stir the mixture into the wok and bring the sauce to a boil, stirring until thickened and clear. Lower the heat and let simmer for 2–3 minutes. Season to taste and serve immediately.

Lamb Couscous

Couscous is a North African specialty. It is usually accompanied by a spicy mixture of meat or sausage with fruit, which adds a note of luxury.

NUTRITIONAL INFORMATION	
Calories 647	Sugars 22g
Protein 41g	Fat 21g
Carbohydrate ...79g	Saturates 6g

20 mins

20 mins

SERVES 4

INGREDIENTS

2 tbsp olive oil

1 lb 2 oz/500 g lean lamb tenderloin, thinly sliced

2 onions, sliced

2 garlic cloves, chopped

1 stick of cinnamon

1 tsp ground ginger

1 tsp paprika

½ tsp chili powder

2½ cups hot chicken bouillon

3 carrots, thinly sliced

2 turnips, halved and sliced

14 oz/400 g canned chopped tomatoes

2 tbsp raisins

15 oz/425 g canned garbanzo beans, drained and rinsed

3 zucchini, sliced

4½ oz/125 g fresh dates, halved and pitted, or 4½ oz/125 g dried apricots

1¾ cups couscous

2½ cups boiling water

salt

1 Heat the oil in a skillet and cook the lamb briskly for 3 minutes, until browned. Remove from the skillet with a slotted spoon, and set aside.

2 Add the onions to the pan and cook, stirring constantly, until soft. Add the garlic and spices and cook for 1 minute.

3 Add the bouillon, carrots, turnips, tomatoes, raisins, garbanzo beans, lamb, and salt to taste. Cover, bring to a boil, and simmer for 12 minutes.

4 Add the zucchini and the dates. Cover again and cook for 8 minutes.

5 Meanwhile, put the couscous in a bowl with 1 teaspoon of salt and pour the boiling water over it. Let it soak for 5 minutes, then fluff it with a fork.

6 To serve, pile the couscous onto a warmed serving platter and make a hollow in the center. Put the meat and vegetables in the hollow, and pour some of the sauce over it. Serve the rest of the sauce separately.

Minty Lamb Kabobs

These spicy lamb kabobs go well with the cool cucumber
and yogurt dip. In the summer you can grill the kabobs outside.

NUTRITIONAL INFORMATION

Calories	295	Sugars	.........4g
Protein	........29g	Fat	..........18g
Carbohydrate	....4g	Saturates	......9g

5 mins   20 mins

SERVES 4

INGREDIENTS

2 tsp coriander seeds

2 tsp cumin seeds

3 cloves

3 green cardamom pods

6 black peppercorns

½-inch/1-cm piece gingerroot

2 garlic cloves

2 tbsp chopped fresh mint

1 small onion, chopped

14 oz/400 g ground lamb

½ tsp salt

lime slices, to serve

DIP

⅔ cup lowfat plain yogurt

2 tbsp chopped fresh mint

3-inch/7.5-cm piece of cucumber, grated

1 tsp mango chutney

1 Heat a skillet and then dry-fry the coriander seeds, cumin seeds, cloves, cardamom pods, and peppercorns, until they turn a shade darker and release a roasted aroma.

2 Grind the spices in a coffee grinder, spice mill, or pestle and mortar.

3 Put the ginger and garlic into a food processor or blender and process to a puree. Add the ground spices, and the mint, onion, lamb, and salt and process until finely chopped. Alternatively, finely chop the garlic and ginger and mix with the ground spices and remaining kabob ingredients.

4 Mold the kabob mixture into small sausage shapes on 4 kabob skewers.

Cook under a preheated hot broiler for 10–15 minutes, turning the skewers occasionally.

5 To make the dip, mix together the yogurt, fresh mint, cucumber, and mango chutney.

6 Serve the kabobs with lime slices and the dip.

Pork with Fennel & Anise

In this dish, lean pork chops, stuffed with an anise and orange filling, are pan-cooked with fennel in an anise-flavored sweet sauce.

NUTRITIONAL INFORMATION

Calories	298	Sugars 10g
Protein	........30g	Fat 10g
Carbohydrate	...18g	Saturates 3g

20 mins   35 mins

SERVES 4

INGREDIENTS

4 lean pork chops, 4½ oz/125 g each

⅓ cup brown rice, cooked

1 tsp orange rind, grated

4 scallions, trimmed and finely chopped

½ tsp anise

1 tbsp olive oil

1 bulb fennel, trimmed and thinly sliced

2 cups unsweetened orange juice

1 tbsp cornstarch

2 tbsp Pernod

salt and pepper

fennel fronds, to garnish

cooked vegetables, to serve

1 Trim away any excess fat from the pork chops. Using a small, sharp knife, make a slit in the center of each chop to create a pocket.

2 Mix the rice, grated orange rind, chopped scallions, seasoning, and anise together in a bowl.

3 Push the rice mixture into the pocket of each chop, then press together gently to seal.

4 Heat the oil in a skillet and cook the pork chops on each side for 2–3 minutes, until lightly browned.

5 Add the sliced fennel and the orange juice to the pan, bring to a boil, and simmer for 15–20 minutes, until the meat is tender and cooked through. Remove the pork and fennel with a slotted spoon and transfer to a serving plate.

6 Blend the cornstarch and Pernod together in a small bowl. Add the cornstarch mixture to the pan and stir into the pan juices. Cook for 2–3 minutes, stirring, until the sauce thickens.

7 Pour the Pernod sauce over the pork chops, garnish with fennel fronds, and serve with some cooked vegetables.

Fruity Pork Skewers

Prunes and apricots bring color and flavor to these tasty pork kabobs.
They are delicious eaten straight off the barbecue grill.

NUTRITIONAL INFORMATION

Calories	205	Sugars	........8g
Protein	........21g	Fat	..........10g
Carbohydrate	....8g	Saturates	......3g

1¼ hrs   15 mins

SERVES 4

I N G R E D I E N T S

4 boneless, lean pork loin steaks

8 ready-to-eat prunes

8 ready-to-eat dried apricots

4 bay leaves

slices of orange and lemon, to garnish

M A R I N A D E

4 tbsp orange juice

2 tbsp olive oil

1 tsp ground bay leaves

salt and pepper

1 Trim the visible fat from the pork and then cut the meat into even-size chunks.

2 Place the pork chunks in a shallow, nonmetallic dish and then add the prunes and apricots.

3 To make the marinade, put the orange juice, oil, and bay leaves in a bowl and mix together. Season to taste with salt and pepper.

4 Pour the marinade over the pork and fruit and toss until well coated. Cover and let marinate in the refrigerator for at least 1 hour or preferably overnight.

5 Soak 4 wooden skewers in cold water to prevent them from catching alight on the barbecue grill.

6 Lift the pork and fruit from the marinade, using a perforated spoon, and reserve the marinade for basting. Thread the pork, fruit, and bay leaves alternately onto the skewers.

7 Grill the skewers on an oiled rack over medium hot coals for 10–15 minutes, turning and basting frequently with the reserved marinade, or until the pork is cooked through. Alternatively, use a broiler

8 Transfer the pork and fruit skewers to warm serving plates. Garnish with slices of orange and lemon and serve hot.

Brown Bread Ice Cream

Although it sounds unusual, this yogurt-based recipe is delicious.
It contains no cream and is ideal for a lowfat diet.

NUTRITIONAL INFORMATION

Calories 264	Sugars 25g	
Protein 12g	Fat 6g	
Carbohydrate . . .43g	Saturates 1g	

2¼ hrs   5 mins

SERVES 4

I N G R E D I E N T S

2½ cups fresh whole-wheat bread crumbs

⅓ cup finely chopped walnuts

4 tbsp superfine sugar

½ tsp ground nutmeg

1 tsp finely grated orange zest

2 cups lowfat unsweetened yogurt

2 large egg whites

TO DECORATE

walnut halves

orange slices

fresh mint

1 Preheat the broiler to medium. Mix together the bread crumbs, walnuts, and sugar and spread over a sheet of foil in the broiler pan.

COOK'S TIP

If you do not have small molds, use ramekins or teacups or, if you prefer, use one large bowl. Alternatively, spoon the mixture into a large, freezerproof container to freeze and serve the ice cream in scoops.

2 Broil the bread crumb mixture, stirring frequently, for 5 minutes, until crisp and evenly browned (take care that the sugar does not burn). Remove from the heat and let cool.

3 When cool, transfer to a mixing bowl and mix in the nutmeg, orange zest, and yogurt. In another bowl, whisk the egg whites until stiff. Gently fold into the bread crumb mixture, using a metal spoon.

4 Spoon the mixture into 4 small molds, smooth over the tops, and freeze for 1½–2 hours, until firm.

5 To serve, hold the bottoms of the molds in hot water for a few seconds, then immediately turn the ice cream out onto serving plates.

6 Serve at once, decorated with the walnuts, oranges, and fresh mint.

Sweet Carrot Halva

This nutritious dessert is bursting with spices, nuts, and raisins.
The nutritional information does not include serving with yogurt.

NUTRITIONAL INFORMATION

Calories ....284 Sugars 33g
Protein ....7g Fat 14g
Carbohydrate ...34g Saturates 3g

10 mins   55 mins

SERVES 6

INGREDIENTS

3½ cups grated carrots

3 cups milk

1 cinnamon stick or piece of cassia
  bark (optional)

4 tbsp vegetable ghee or oil

5 tbsp granulated sugar

⅓ cup chopped unsalted pistachios

4 tbsp blanched almonds,
  slivered or chopped

½ cup seedless raisins

8 cardamom pods, split and seeds removed
  and crushed

thick plain yogurt, to serve

1 Put the grated carrots, milk, and cinnamon or cassia, if using, into a large, heavy pan and bring to a boil. Reduce the heat to very low and simmer, uncovered, for 35–40 minutes, or until the mixture is thick (with no milk remaining). Stir the mixture frequently during cooking to prevent it from sticking.

2 Remove and discard the cinnamon or cassia. Heat the ghee or oil in a nonstick skillet, add the carrot mixture, and stir-fry over medium heat for about 5 minutes, or until the carrots take on a glossy sheen.

3 Add the sugar, pistachios, almonds, raisins, and crushed cardamom seeds, mix thoroughly, and continue stir-frying for another 3–4 minutes. Serve warm or cold with thick plain yogurt.

COOK'S TIP
The quickest and easiest way to grate this quantity of carrots is by using a food processor fitted with the appropriate blade.

Aromatic Fruit Salad

The fruits in this salad are arranged attractively on serving plates with a spicy syrup spooned over them.

NUTRITIONAL INFORMATION	
Calories 125	Sugars 29g
Protein 3g	Fat 1g
Carbohydrate . . .29g	Saturates 0.2g

25 mins   5 mins

SERVES 6

INGREDIENTS

3½ tbsp granulated sugar

⅔ cup water

1 cinnamon stick or large piece of cassia bark

4 cardamom pods, crushed

1 clove

juice of 1 orange

juice of 1 lime

½ honeydew melon

large wedge of watermelon

2 ripe guavas

3 ripe nectarines

about 18 strawberries

a little toasted shredded coconut, for sprinkling

sprigs of mint or rose petals, to decorate

strained lowfat unsweetened yogurt, for serving

1 First prepare the syrup. Put the sugar, water, cinnamon, cardamom pods, and clove into a pan and bring to a boil, stirring to dissolve the sugar. Simmer for 2 minutes, then remove from the heat.

2 Add the orange juice and lime juice to the syrup. Let cool and infuse while preparing the fruits.

3 Peel and remove the seeds from the honeydew melon and watermelon and cut the flesh into neat slices.

4 Cut the guavas in half, scoop out the seeds, then peel carefully and slice the flesh neatly.

5 Cut the nectarines into slices and hull and slice the strawberries.

6 Arrange the slices of fruit attractively on 6 serving plates.

7 Strain the prepared cooled syrup and spoon over the sliced fruits.

8 Sprinkle the fruit salad with a little toasted coconut. Decorate each serving with sprigs of mint or rose petals and serve with yogurt.